DATE DUE

DEC 1 1 2012		
DEC 2 0 2012		
MAR 0 5 2012		
MAR 2 7 2013		
MAR 2 7 2013		
OCT 2 7 2015		
JAN 2 0 2016		
SEP 0 7 2016		
OCT 0 7 2016		
SEP 1 3 2017		
DEC 1 9		
SEP 2 5		

Demco

D1068882

Fantastic Feats

by David Orme

Perfection Learning®

Fantastic Feats
by David Orme
Educational consultant: Helen Bird
Illustrated by Martin Bolchover

Image Credits

'Get the Facts' section - images copyright: U.S. Air Force/Ashely Silvey; Jan Rihak; Marc Summers; Brian Sullivan; Aidan Jones; Giorgio Brugnoni; Patrick Herrera; Ransom Publishing.

Every effort has been made to locate all copyright holders of material used in this book. If any errors or omissions have occurred, corrections will be made in future editions of this book.

www.perfectionlearning.com

1 2 3 4 5 6 7 PP 17 16 15 14 13 12
PP/Logan, Iowa, USA
2/12

26886

RLB ISBN-13: 978-1-61384-023-8
RLB ISBN-10: 1-61384-023-3

PB ISBN-13: 978-0-7891-8243-2
PB ISBN-10: 0-7891-8243-2

Printed in the United States of America

Table of Contents

Fantastic Feats

Get **the** facts

Amazing feats

Do you enjoy a challenge?

Or do you say . . .

I can't do that!

COULD YOU . . .

- climb Mount Everest?
- eat 17 pounds of cow brains in fifteen minutes?
- jump through fire?

The famous tight-rope walker **Blondin** achieved one of the greatest feats of all time. In 1859, he crossed **Niagara Falls** on a tightrope.

Blondin!

Then he did it again— on a **bicycle**!

And again— carrying someone on his back!

Cup of tea, anyone?

Once he stopped in the middle—to cook his **breakfast!**

DON'T TRY THIS AT HOME!

How tough are you?

What do you have to do to become . . .

THE WORLD'S STRONGEST PERSON?

? **Carry a huge rock called a Husafell Stone?** *(Don't drop it on your feet.)*

? **Lift a car?** *(This is called a dead lift.)*

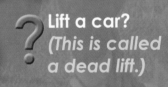

Walk carrying heavy weights?
(This is called a farmer's walk.)

DON'T
TRY THIS . . .
oh, you know where!

Pull a truck 100 meters along the road?
(Hope they've taken the brakes off!)

Mr. Memory

Look at the pictures
below for 30 seconds.

ONE
YOU *CAN*
TRY AT HOME

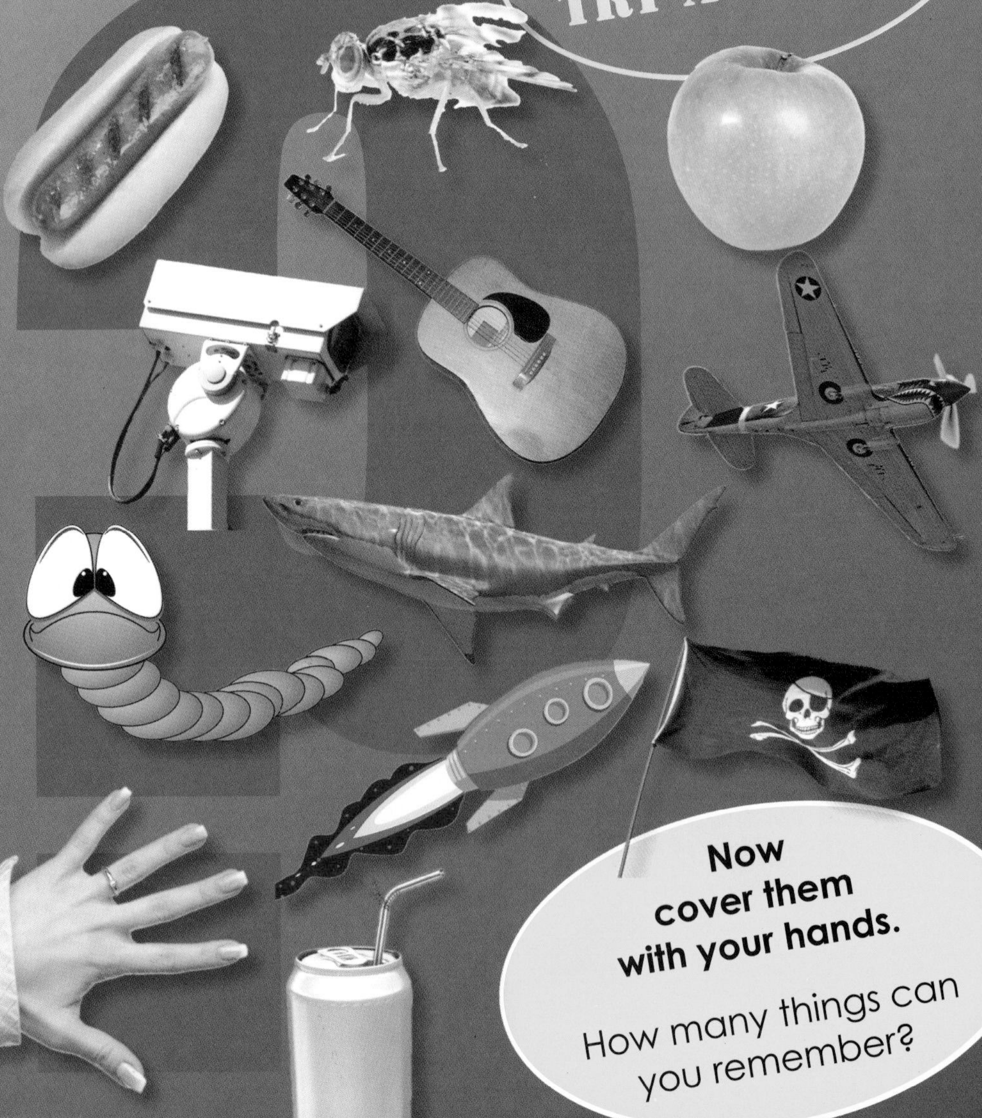

**Now
cover them
with your hands.**

How many things can
you remember?

Now look at the numbers below for **30 seconds.**

Then close the book and see how many you can remember—in the right order!

```
3.1415926535897932384626433832795
  02884197169399375105820974944592 3
  07164062862089986280348253421170 6
  79442881097566593344612847564823 3
  78678316527120190914564856692346 0
  34861045432664821339360726024914 1
  27372458700660631558817488152092 0
```

TOUGH, EH?

But not for Mr. **Akira Haraguchi** of Japan.

Mr. Haraguchi remembered these 230 numbers, **plus 99,770 more!**

Halfway through saying them, he forgot where he was— so he started again!

Umm...

Do you think Mr. Haraguchi ever forgets his phone number?

Climbing Mount Everest

This is the **ultimate challenge**.

Many people have died trying to climb this mountain. By the end of 2011, 225 people had died trying to reach the top.

You can get trapped or lost because of bad weather.

The top 4,000 feet is called the **Death Zone**. There isn't enough oxygen in the air. Without extra oxygen, your body will collapse after a few days.

On May 15, 2005, **Mark Inglis** made it to the top of Everest.

SO WHAT?

In 1982, Mark had been climbing in New Zealand.

He was trapped in an ice cave.

When he was rescued, he had frostbite in his legs. Both legs were **amputated** (cut off) below the knee.

That didn't stop him from tackling the world's greatest challenge.

THAT'S WHAT!

DEATH ZONE

Not so amazing?

Some feats look absolutely amazing.

How would you like to **walk on fire**?

Or lie on a **bed of nails** and let someone put a **block** on your **stomach** and **smash it** with a **hammer**?

How do they do it?

Firewalking

Wow! Amazing feet!

The ash from the burning charcoal or wood stops the worst of the heat from reaching your feet.

If you walk across quickly, the soles of your feet will help insulate you. Water or sweat on your feet can protect you.

But the fire has to be just right for it to work, so **leave it to the experts!**

DON'T TRY THIS AT HOME!

Why don't the nails hurt? Because there are lots of them.

Bed of Nails

If you sit on one nail, the whole weight of your body will press down on it. **Ow!**

If you lie on **hundreds of nails**, each one only has to carry a little bit of you. This isn't enough to break your skin.

The **hard part** is lying down and getting up again! **Be very careful!**

What about breaking blocks?

Make sure the blocks are made of **crumbly stone**. This will soak up the force from the hammer.

15

Crazy and not so crazy

Crazy eating

Takeru Kobayashi just loves eating; in fact, he is the eating champ (or **chump**) of the world! Takeru was born with an unusual stomach. This helps him **stuff down** huge amounts of food.

In 2002, he ate more than 17 pounds of cow brains in fifteen minutes!

In 2011, he set the **world hot dog eating record**, eating 69 hot dogs in 10 minutes.

Michael Lotito is known as *Monsieur Mangetout*, which is French for "Mr. Eat Everything!"

Monsieur Mangetout has eaten bicycles, TV sets, and shopping carts. Between 1978 and 1980, **he ate an entire airplane**.

Human birdmen

People have always wanted to **fly like birds**. Until 2008, every year in Bognor, England, birdmen tried to fly by jumping off a pier.

No one has managed it yet!

This picture shows the German birdman, **Otto Lilienthal**, in 1896.

It looks like a crazy stunt, but Otto's work was used to design hang gliders and even aircraft.

Feat
of
Endurance

Chapter 1
Alone

The first thing that hit Ron was the heat. Within seconds, his clothes were damp with sweat.

Ron moved deeper into the rain forest, following a small stream. The noises got louder.

Woods and forests at home were quiet places. Here in the rain forest, it was as noisy as a big city. There was the buzz of insects, the screaming of birds high overhead, and the call of monkeys. At least, Ron guessed they were monkeys.

Ron was used to the big city with streets full of shops and coffeehouses and with people all around.

Here, Ron was alone. The boat had gone. Ron had been dumped on the edge of a great river. He had the clothes he was wearing and not much else.

Somehow, he had to survive.

Chapter 2
Hungry!

Ron sat down on a rock and checked his pockets. Matches. They would be useful. A knife. A bar of chocolate that was already melting. There was no point in keeping that, so he ate it.

He heard a crashing sound in the forest. It was getting closer and closer. Ron knew there weren't many large animals in the rain forest. But just in case, he broke off a branch and sharpened the end.

Now he had a spear!

Water wasn't going to be a problem if he kept close to the stream. But what about food? There was fruit in the forest, but it might be poisonous.

Through the trees he saw a flock of parrots eating bright yellow fruit. It didn't poison them, so Ron ate it.

But fruit didn't fill him up. He still felt hungry.

Chapter 3
The rain forest at night

Ron thought lighting a fire would be easy. It wasn't. Everything was damp. It took half of his matches to get a fire going.

He was really hungry now.

Ron got up to put more wood on the fire. He felt something moving under his foot. Then he felt a sudden pain in his ankle.

He looked down and found he was standing on a snake—and the snake had just bitten him!

The snake was ready to strike again. Ron grabbed his spear and stabbed at the snake. By pure luck, he managed to kill it.

But was he hungry enough to eat a snake?

Chapter 4
Poisoned!

Ron chopped up the snake and cooked it on a stick. It didn't just taste bad—it was much, much worse than that.

Then Ron noticed his leg was swelling up. Poison! He began to feel dizzy. His heart started to pound.

Suddenly, there was a bright light, and a face looked down at him.

Ron lay back in the hospital bed. The producer of the *Feat of Endurance* reality TV show was there.

"I failed, didn't I?" said Ron.

"No, you didn't! You're alive, Ron, so you did better than the other contestants! In a couple of days, you'll be ready for your next "feat of endurance!"

Two days later, Ron was shivering at the North Pole. All he had was a knife and a box of matches.